ACCIDENTAL SCIENTIFIC DISCOVERIES THAT CHANGED THE WORLD

OOPS! IT'S PLASTIC!

BY META MANCHESTER

Gareth Stevens
PUBLISHING

Please visit our website, www.garethstevens.com. For a free color catalog of all our high-quality books, call toll free 1-800-542-2595 or fax 1-877-542-2596.

Library of Congress Cataloging-in-Publication Data

Names: Manchester, Meta, author.
Title: Oops! it's plastic! / Meta Manchester.
Other titles: Oops! It is plastic | It's plastic | It is plastic
Description: New York : Gareth Stevens Publishing, [2020] | Series:
   Accidental scientific discoveries that changed the world
Identifiers: LCCN 2018050183| ISBN 9781538239940 (pbk.) | ISBN 9781538239964
   (library bound) | ISBN 9781538239957 (6 pack)
Subjects: LCSH: Plastics–Juvenile literature. | Discoveries in
   science–Juvenile literature.
Classification: LCC TP1125 .M36 2020 | DDC 668.4–dc23
LC record available at https://lccn.loc.gov/2018050183

First Edition

Published in 2020 by
Gareth Stevens Publishing
111 East 14th Street, Suite 349
New York, NY 10003

Copyright © 2020 Gareth Stevens Publishing

Designer: Katelyn E. Reynolds
Editor: Monika Davies

Photo credits: Cover, p. 1 Tetra Images/Getty Images; cover, pp. 1–32 (burst) jirawat phueksriphan/Shutterstock.com; cover, pp. 1–32 (burst lines) KID_A/Shutterstock.com; p. 5 (bottles) Scisetti Alfio/Shutterstock.com; p. 5 (blocks) Seregam/Shutterstock.com; p. 5 (straws) matkub2499/Shutterstock.com; p. 7 (both) molekuul_be/Shutterstock.com; p. 9 Kirn Vintage Stock/Corbis via Getty Images; p. 11 VK Studio/Shutterstock.com; pp. 13, 17, 22, 23, Bettmann/Getty Images; p. 15 (inset) Science History Institute (https://www.sciencehistory.org/)/Mary Mark Ockerbloom/Wikipedia.org; pp. 15 (main), 21 SSPL/Getty Images; p. 16 Steve Russell/Toronto Star via Getty Images; p. 19 padu_foto/Shutterstock.com; p. 25 (top) PrairieEyes/Shutterstock.com; p. 25 (bottom) Suzanne Tucker/Shutterstock.com.

Printed in the United States of America

CPSIA compliance information: Batch #CS19GS: For further information contact Gareth Stevens, New York, New York at 1-800-542-2595.

CONTENTS

Words in the glossary appear in **bold** type the first time they are used in the text.

PLASTIC ALL AROUND US

Take a look around you. How many items do you spy that are made of plastic? You probably see quite a few, like your pen, water bottle, or bags from the grocery store. Plastic is everywhere! It's a hard **material** to imagine life without. However, until just over 100 years ago, plastic as we know it today didn't exist.

Some types of plastic were invented accidentally by scientists who were trying to make something else. They had no idea that their accidental inventions would go on to change the world in ways both big and small!

How "Plastic" Came To Be

THE WORD "PLASTIC" COMES FROM THE GREEK WORD *PLASTIKOS*, MEANING "ABLE TO BE **MOLDED**." TODAY, THE WORD PLASTIC MEANS A LIGHT, **DURABLE** MATERIAL THAT CAN BE FORMED AND PRESSED INTO MANY DIFFERENT SHAPES. LEO HENDRIK BAEKELAND, ONE OF THE ACCIDENTAL INVENTORS OF PLASTIC, FIRST USED THE WORD "PLASTIC" WITH THIS MEANING IN 1909.

Plastic is a common material for everyday items. Every minute, almost a million plastic drink bottles are sold worldwide.

5

WHAT IS PLASTIC?

Plastics are all made up of the same group of materials called polymers. Polymers are long repeating chains of carbon molecules, or very small pieces of matter. These chains can slip past each other easily. This is what makes plastic moldable.

There are two types of plastic: natural and **synthetic**. Natural plastic is found in nature, and examples include animal horns and natural rubber. Synthetic plastic is usually man-made. We use a lot of synthetic plastic in our day-to-day lives.

Synthetic plastic is useful because it doesn't have a **chemical reaction** with other materials. This means we can use this kind of plastic to store chemicals, like gasoline or soap, without the container melting.

THE PROBLEM WITH PLASTIC

PLASTIC DOESN'T BREAK DOWN EASILY, BECAUSE IT DOESN'T REACT CHEMICALLY WITH MOST MATERIALS. THIS MEANS PLASTIC TAKES A VERY LONG TIME TO GO AWAY! IT'LL STAY IN THE NATURAL WORLD FOR MANY YEARS. TO PROTECT OUR ENVIRONMENT, IT'S IMPORTANT FOR US TO USE LESS PLASTIC, AS WELL AS RECYCLE PLASTIC.

Synthetic plastic can be molded into almost any shape you can imagine, because plastic polymers slip smoothly past each other—like strands of spaghetti!

POLYMER

POLYMER CHAIN

LIFE BEFORE PLASTIC

Today, plastic items are found everywhere. But, plastic has only been used as a material for about the last 100 years. Before, people stored liquids in glass or metal containers. Plates and bowls were made of china or ceramic, which is clay that has hardened. Silverware was made of metal. Some people even used natural items, like banana leaves, as plates.

Our way of living was also different before the invention of plastic. Most meals were made at home, so we didn't use travel containers for food. Items like baby diapers and shopping bags were made of cloth, so they could be used again and again.

REUSABLE BAGS

EACH YEAR, AMERICANS THROW AWAY AROUND 100 BILLION PLASTIC BAGS. IT CAN TAKE ANYWHERE FROM 10 TO 1,000 YEARS FOR PLASTIC BAGS TO BREAK DOWN. PLASTIC BAGS ARE STILL AVAILABLE AT MANY STORES. HOWEVER, MANY PEOPLE ARE NOW USING REUSABLE GROCERY BAGS INSTEAD. THEY CHOOSE REUSABLE BAGS TO CUT DOWN THEIR IMPACT ON THE ENVIRONMENT.

This family in the early 1900s likely wouldn't have kept leftovers from dinner like we do. Today, many people use plastic containers to store leftover food from our meals in the fridge or freezer.

BRILLIANT BAKELITE

In the early 1900s, more and more electrical items, such as lights, were manufactured in the United States. These electrical items had wires, which needed to be **insulated**. This made sure people wouldn't get electrocuted, or killed with an electric shock, if they touched the wires.

Shellac was the material used for electrical insulation. It's a natural form of plastic. Shellac is a type of resin, or sticky substance, made by the lac insect. At the time, it was the only material used for electrical insulation. However, shellac was expensive and hard to get. Scientists—including Belgian-born scientist Leo Hendrik Baekeland—began trying to create a **substitute** for shellac.

A Long Process

SHELLAC IS MADE USING BEETLES FROM ASIA. THE EAST ASIAN LAC INSECT COVERS TREE BRANCHES WITH A **SECRETION** THAT HARDENS. WORKERS HAD TO CUT DOWN THE TREE BRANCHES, SCRAPE THE SECRETION OFF, AND WASH THE SECRETION TO REMOVE BUG PARTS. THEN, THE SHELLAC WAS READY FOR USE.

In the early 1900s, gramophones were a popular electrical item sold in the United States. These were record players that played music. Shellac was used as an electrical insulation for gramophones.

Since the early 1900s, Baekeland had been trying to create a substitute for shellac that was cheaper and easier to make. In 1907, he was working in his research **laboratory** in Yonkers, New York, when he chanced upon a big discovery.

Baekeland tried mixing and heating different chemicals to make a shellac substitute. Then, one day, he mixed two chemicals: formaldehyde and phenol. These two chemicals mixed together didn't quite make shellac. But, Baekeland realized the mixture made something even better.

The material Baekeland made was moldable when warm. The material then hardened when it cooled. When the material was put under high heat and extreme pressure, it stayed permanently molded!

THERMO-WHAT?

BAKELITE WAS THE FIRST MAN-MADE THERMOSETTING PLASTIC. THERMOSETTING PLASTIC DOESN'T SOFTEN WHEN HEATED. THIS WAS DIFFERENT THAN NATURAL PLASTICS, SUCH AS SHELLAC, WHICH WOULD BECOME SOFT IF IT BECAME TOO WARM OUTSIDE. THIS OPENED UP OPPORTUNITIES TO MAKE NEW KINDS OF ITEMS, SINCE BAKELITE WAS LONG-LASTING AND NOT AFFECTED BY HEAT.

Baekeland was born in Ghent, Belgium. He went to the University of Ghent where he studied chemistry and physics. In 1889, Baekeland and his wife moved to America.

Baekeland's new material was durable. It did not break, catch fire, or react with other chemicals. Baekeland had accidentally created the first completely synthetic plastic. He named this new material for himself: Bakelite.

In 1909, Baekeland's application for a **patent** for Bakelite was accepted. This meant no one else could use Baekeland's process to make Bakelite for a time. Then, in 1910, Baekeland founded the General Bakelite Company to sell the material. The company called Bakelite the "material of a thousand uses."

Bakelite could be molded into almost any shape. This made Bakelite a useful material to make many household items, such as buttons, televisions, washing machine parts, and light bulb sockets.

THE BAKELIZER

BAEKELAND CREATED A SPECIAL IRON MACHINE TO MAKE BAKELITE, WHICH HE NAMED THE "BAKELIZER." EARLY USERS NICKNAMED IT "OLD FAITHFUL" BECAUSE THE MACHINE WORKED SO WELL. TODAY, THE FIRST BAKELIZER IS OWNED BY THE NATIONAL MUSEUM OF AMERICAN HISTORY AT THE SMITHSONIAN INSTITUTION.
THE MACHINE IS STILL IN WORKING CONDITION!

Electricity couldn't flow through Bakelike, so it was used to insulate electrical parts. Bakelite was used to make the case for this television around 1950.

BAKELITE

BAKELIZER

15

However, starting in 1926, Baekeland's patents began to expire, or end. This meant other people and companies could begin making products like Bakelite. Soon, there were too many kinds of plastic to count! For example, vinyl was one of the new plastics to hit the market. The first vinyl items included golf balls and shoe heels.

At the time, Bakelite products were expensive. However, with all of the new plastic products on the market, the cost of plastic went down. More and more, plastic became the material of choice. This marked the beginning of the "age of plastics," which continues to today.

BAKELITE JEWELRY

BAKELITE JEWELRY

BAKELITE JEWELRY WAS POPULAR IN THE 1930S AND 1940S. BAKELITE JEWELRY WAS USUALLY BRIGHTLY COLORED. THE JEWELRY ALSO HAD FUN DESIGNS, SUCH AS POLKA DOTS OR TINY PINEAPPLES. TODAY, OLD BAKELITE JEWELRY IS VALUABLE, OR WORTH A LOT OF MONEY, BECAUSE IT'S NOT MADE ANYMORE. THE COST OF BAKELITE JEWELRY CAN BE OVER $1,000!

Leo Baekeland (left) is holding the first tube of Bakelite ever made. In 1939, Baekeland retired and sold the General Bakelite Company to the Union Carbide Company for $16.5 million.

CREATING POLYETHYLENE

After Bakelite was created, another type of plastic would change the world. It was also made accidentally! In 1899, German scientist Hans von Pechmann was completing an experiment. At the end, he saw a waxy, white material at the bottom of a test tube. He wrote down what he saw and then cleaned the test tube. At the time, the material didn't seem useful.

Von Pechmann had no idea he'd accidentally made a type of plastic calld polyethylene (pol-ee-ETH-uh-leen). It would be many more years before anyone would realize what this material could do. Today, it's one of the most common types of plastic in the world!

What's in a Name?

POLYETHYLENE GETS ITS NAME FROM HOW IT'S MADE. THIS KIND OF PLASTIC IS CREATED WHEN A CHEMICAL CALLED ETHYLENE GOES THROUGH A PROCESS CALLED POLYMERIZATION. THIS IS THE MAKING OF LONG, REPEATING CHAINS OF POLYMERS. THIS PROCESS CREATES A SIMPLE AND CHEAP PLASTIC, WHICH IS WHY IT'S USED TO MAKE MANY ITEMS.

Today, polyethylene is used for plastic bags because the material is thin and bends easily. This kind of plastic is also recyclable.

Then, in 1933, British scientists Eric Fawcett and Reginald Gibson accidentally created the same material. The two scientists were trying to react ethylene, a gas, with benzaldehyde, a liquid, under high pressure. However, their tools weren't working properly. Instead, they created the same waxy material as von Pechmann had years before.

Fawcett and Gibson were both part of the Imperial Chemical Industries company. The company began perfecting the way to make polyethylene. In 1938, ICI started producing polyethylene on a larger scale. It became one of the first plastics made in factories. By 1939, at the start of World War II, large amounts of polyethylene were being made.

POLYETHYLENE IN WWII

THIS NEW FORM OF PLASTIC WAS AN IMPORTANT MATERIAL DURING WORLD WAR II. IT WAS USED AS INSULATION FOR RADAR, A MACHINE THAT USES RADIO WAVES TO FIND AND IDENTIFY OBJECTS. THIS FORM OF PLASTIC WAS LIGHT, WHICH MEANT RADARS COULD BE PUT ON AIRPLANES WITHOUT INCREASING THE WEIGHT OF THE PLANE.

This is one of the first pieces of polyethylene made by ICI in 1938. The material was first used by ICI to make a walking stick!

Although other scientists discovered and created polyethylene, German scientist Karl Ziegler often gets the credit for inventing it. In 1953, Ziegler found certain metals could catalyze, or cause, the making of polyethylene at room temperature. Before, polyethylene could only be made using high temperatures and pressure.

While Ziegler wasn't the first to invent polyethylene, he made it cheaper and easier to make. This thin, soft plastic has been used in many ways over the years. Polyethylene is the material used to make many toys, plastic food wrap, pipes, thick containers, and gas tanks for cars.

KARL ZIEGLER

A "Hoop" Demand

POLYETHYLENE IS ALSO THE MATERIAL BEHIND THE PLASTIC HULA HOOP! IN 1958, THE COMPANY WHAM-O BEGAN USING POLYETHYLENE TO CREATE COLORFUL HOOPS. THEY SOLD 25 MILLION HULA HOOPS IN THE FIRST 4 MONTHS OF SALES. THIS CREATED A HUGE DEMAND FOR THE PRODUCTION OF POLYETHYLENE. THESE EARLY HULA HOOPS COST $1.98 EACH.

In 1963, Karl Ziegler and Giulio Natta, an Italian scientist, shared the Nobel Prize for Chemistry for their discoveries and work with polyethylene.

GIULIO NATTA

23

PLASTIC IMPROVEMENTS

A lot has changed since Bakelite and polyethylene were invented. Plastic has become even easier to produce and is used in many ways. Plastic packaging keeps food fresh and keeps it from spoiling, or going bad. It's lightweight, so plastic is often used to make car parts, which lighten the car so it uses less gasoline. Seat belts are also made of plastic.

Of course, plastics are also used to make electronics, such as phones, which has changed the way humans keep in touch with each other. Plastics can be used to make prosthetic, or fake, limbs for people who need them, too. Our lives would be very different without plastics!

PLASTIC AT THE DOCTOR'S OFFICE

PLASTIC IS ESPECIALLY IMPORTANT IN MEDICINE. IT'S USED TO MAKE SINGLE-USE ITEMS, SUCH AS GLOVES AND NEEDLES, WHICH HELP KEEP DISEASES FROM SPREADING. PLASTIC MEDICINE BOTTLES KEEP MEDICINE FRESH AND SAFE TO TAKE. PLASTIC IS EVEN USED AS A THIN LAYER TO COVER PILLS!

Plastic is used to make athletic gear, such as shin pads and helmets. This gear helps athletes perform their best and keeps them safe.

PLASTIC PROBLEMS

Plastic has unfortunately become a problem in our environment. Sometimes, people don't get rid of plastic by recycling it. This means that the plastic ends up in landfills or the natural world.

When plastic isn't properly recycled, it can end up in the ocean, where it's a danger to animals. Sea animals might eat the plastic or get tangled up in it. Plastic that's thrown away—and not recycled—can leak chemicals into the ground and water. These chemicals can make people and animals sick. Luckily, there's a lot you can do to keep plastic from becoming pollution!

PLASTIC-EATING ENZYMES

SCIENTISTS HAVE FOUND AN ENZYME THAT CAN "EAT" PLASTIC. ENZYMES SPEED UP CHEMICAL REACTIONS. THIS PLASTIC-EATING ENZYME CAN QUICKEN THE BREAKDOWN OF PLASTIC. SCIENTISTS ARE STILL LEARNING ABOUT THIS ENZYME, BUT THEY'RE WORKING HARD TO FIGURE OUT HOW TO MAKE IT PART OF OUR RECYCLING PROCESS.

There are many ways we can cut down plastic pollution. Can you think of other ways you can help?

USE PAPER STRAWS INSTEAD OF PLASTIC STRAWS.

CARRY A REUSABLE BOTTLE TO FILL UP WITH WATER WHILE YOU'RE ON THE GO.

RECYCLE AT HOME AND AT SCHOOL.

WHAT CAN I DO?

BRING REUSABLE BAGS TO THE GROCERY STORE TO CARRY YOUR ITEMS.

START AN ENVIRONMENTAL CLUB AT SCHOOL AND SPREAD AWARENESS ABOUT PLASTIC POLLUTION.

USE METAL OR GLASS CONTAINERS TO TAKE FOOD WITH YOU, INSTEAD OF COVERING YOUR FOOD WITH PLASTIC WRAP.

PICK UP GARBAGE AND RECYCLE PLASTIC WHEN YOU SEE IT ON THE STREET.

A WORLD FULL OF PLASTIC

Plastic has changed the world in good and bad ways. Plastic has helped us create items that make our lives easier. However, plastic has caused a lot of pollution in our world. One thing is for sure, though—our lives wouldn't be the same without plastic. Pay attention to how much of what you use is made of plastic. Can you imagine how different life would be without it?

It's incredible that such an important material was invented accidentally—and by many different people! Who knows? Maybe the next amazing type of plastic will also be an accidental discovery.

New Plastics of the Future?

Polylactic acid (PLA) is made from a chemical called lactic acid. Scientists get lactic acid from corn! This kind of plastic doesn't take as long to break down in the environment. For example, if a PLA bottle gets left behind in the ocean, it would take 6 months to 2 years to break down versus around 450 years for a regular plastic bottle.

> Plastic is now used in almost every industry, but it has a fairly short history. What do you think the future holds for plastic?

PLASTIC PROGRESS

1899 — German scientist Hans von Pechmann creates polyethylene and throws it away.

1907 — Leo Hendrik Baekeland creates Bakelite in his research laboratory in New York.

1910 — Baekeland founds the General Bakelite Company to sell Bakelite.

1926 — Baekeland's patents begin to expire. Other plastic makers begin to crowd the market.

1933 — Eric Fawcett and Reginald Gibson accidentally make polyethylene.

1938 — Polyethylene is one of the first plastics made in factories.

1953 — Karl Ziegler figures out a way to catalyze polyethylene at room temperature.

Current — Since the 1950s, we have made almost 9 billion tons of plastic.

GLOSSARY

chemical reaction: a process in which one or more kinds of matter change to one or more other kinds of matter because of coming into contact with one another

durable: able to last

insulate: to surround something to prevent heat, electricity, or sound from passing through

laboratory: a place with tools to perform experiments

material: matter from which something is made or can be made

mold: to form or press something into a certain shape

patent: an official document that gives a person the rights to a design, machine, or process for a time

secretion: the product of a living thing that's given off to perform a specific useful function in the living thing

substitute: a thing that takes the place of someone or something else

synthetic: made by combining different substances; not natural

FOR MORE INFORMATION

BOOKS

Maloof, Torrey. *We Recycle*. Huntington Beach, CA: Teacher Created Materials, 2015.

Moser, Elise. *What Milly Did: The Remarkable Pioneer of Plastics Recycling*. Toronto, ON: Groundwood Books, 2016.

Newman, Patricia. *Plastic, Ahoy!: Investigating the Great Pacific Garbage Patch*. Minneapolis, MN: Millbrook Press, 2014.

WEBSITES

Recycle This!
www.climatekids.nasa.gov/recycle-this
Find out more about what you can recycle.

Plastic Pollution
kids.nationalgeographic.com/explore/nature/kids-vs-plastic/pollution
Learn about the problems around single-use plastic.

Who Invented Plastic?
www.wonderopolis.org/wonder/who-invented-plastic
Learn about the different scientists who created plastics—accidentally and on purpose!

INDEX